(rustle rustle)
THUMP THUMP

Poems by R. Nikolas Macioci

Kung Fu Treachery Press
Rancho Cucamonga, CA

Copyright © R. Nikolas Macioci, 2020
First Edition 1 3 5 7 9 10 8 6 4 2
ISBN: 978-1-950380-85-5
LCCN: 2020930940

Design, edits and layout: John T. Keehan, Jr.
Cover and title page images: Jon Lee Grafton
Author photo: R. Nikolas Macioci
All rights reserved. No part of this publication may be reproduced or transmitted in any form or by any means, electronic or mechanical, including photocopying, recording or by info retrieval system, without prior written permission from the author.

ACKNOWLEDGMENTS:

Grateful acknowledgment is made to *Chiron Review* in which "Necks" and "Open Mic" first appeared.

TABLE OF CONTENTS

Bobby Barebutt / 1

I'm Thrilled Everytime I Show My Boxers / 3

Rustle Rustle Thump Thump / 5

My Catholic Boyhood / 7

Uses of a Homemade Telescope / 8

Catatonic / 9

Dogmatic / 11

Guns Galore / 13

Something to Do With Raccoons / 14

Dear Louise / 16

In the Parlor / 18

Amorous Advice / 20

Wrong Turn / 22

Aunt Candy Captivates the Nursing Home / 24

Haircut / 26

A Modesty Proposal / 28

Poem Killers / 29

Words by which We Are Known / 31

A Poet's Prerogative / 33

Waiting Room / 34

My Life As a Songbird / 35

Demolition Derby / 36

Substitute Mailman / 37

A Murderous Poet / 39

Spare Part / 41

Vocal Music Class / 43

Media Mess / 45

Asbestos / 47

The Value in Waiting to Die / 49

Talking to God / 51

Octogenarian One-Step / 53

First Flight / 54

Time Out / 56

A Little Walk Never Hurt Anyone / 58

Dog in the Rain / 60

Open Mic / 62

Logistics of Buying a New Car / 64

Pride and Perspiration / 66

Bargain Rate / 68

Clean / 70

At War With White Castle / 71

Lessons in Satisfaction / 73

Moby's / 75

Necks / 76

How to Survive in the Hospital / 77

Don't Touch the Cows / 78

Destination Goodwill / 80

God Loves Groundhogs / 82

*If you could choose one
characteristic that would get you
through life, choose a sense of humor*
                        -Jennifer Jones

*Humor is just common sense,
dancing*
                        -William James

For Sandra Ditschle, faithful friend and closet editor.
Thanks for your support and encouragement.

BOBBY BAREBUTT

Bobby is a nudist. He is also a friend.
In fact, he is a friendly nudist. His
men's club meets once a week at
public places that have been privately
rented so that the congregation can
cavort without attire.

Bowling in the nude, anyone? Oh yes,
that is something he has done. Standing
erect and carefully aiming his balls,
seen from behind, he added new meaning
to the term split.

Among other activities requiring bare
essentials have been camping and cocktail
parties. I wouldn't touch the latter in this poem
with a ten foot pole or whatever.

He's very fond of my poetry. In fact he
keeps track of my readings and sometimes
edits my work. Occasionally, his group
holds book club meetings with special speakers.
He has invited me to be a reader at such
an event with the qualification that I do
it in the nude. On hearing this I almost

onamonapia-ed in my pants. He has tried
to soft talk me into it several times,
guaranteeing that after several minutes
I would be perfectly comfortable. I refused
on the basis of modesty and not because
I couldn't figure out what not to wear.

It's understandable that the group's repertoire
has never included tennis or trampoline.
Although the night they rented the pizza
parlor, the chef wanted to know if they
preferred penis or pepperoni.

I haven't seen Bobby for a while, but
he was planning a nude Caribbean cruise
on a ship called Ceaseless Fun. I reminded
him not to forget sunscreen and that I would
be at the dock with a welcome home gift
of designer socks.

I'M THRILLED EVERYTIME I SHOW MY BOXERS

I'm proud of my 99 cent boxers
bought at the thrift store. I stumbled onto
them by accident. At first I thought
they were a plaid placemat and wondered
where the other three were until I saw
the pee hole. The very looseness of the legs
fascinated me. How could I possibly
get all that material tucked into my pants
without looking obscene and bulgy.
I was used to the elastic leg holes
in briefs cutting off the circulation
in my thighs and grabbing my crotch
like a delinquent hand. How could all
this freedom offer sufficient support.
I may as well be naked. Plus, when I
grew up the only men I ever saw in boxers
were men whose potbellys extended
waistbands twelve inches beyond
the designated size. I considered
boxers to be old men's underwear.

Recently, however, when I was shopping
in Kohl's with my hand on a six pack
of briefs, like a call from heaven, my eye
caught row after row of GQ men slimmed into
multi-patterned and multicolored boxers.

At that moment I had an underwear
epiphany. I'd always thought of myself
as fairly fashionable, and since I'd never
taken my clothes off in public, I'd never
experienced underwear condemnation.
I had fallen behind the times. All of this
came to mind as I held the blue plaid boxers
in my hand in the middle of the thrift store.

I bought them and two dozen more after
combing all the thrift stores in central
Ohio. They've changed my life, given
me confidence I'd never had. I wear them
down the long driveway to the mailbox
every morning, answer the door in them, and
wear them to clean house. Currently, with
the addition of a t-shirt, I'm contemplating
my first trip to Kroger. I just haven't decided
whether the appropriate footwear would be
sneakers or flip-flops.

RUSTLE RUSTLE THUMP THUMP

Rustle rustle thump thump.
Someone's in the attic. The sound is loud.
Whoever is crawling around has traded
secrecy for determination, is bold as a bear
on its hind legs, presumptuous as a jewel thief.

Meanwhile, it's raining enough to attract ducks,
and ducks might end up floating around
in my kitchen where a leak has sprung in the ceiling.
The metronomic drip combined with the thump
weirds me out.

I shove a wastebasket under the leak.
Drip changes to plop. The prowler in the attic
persists romping from rafter to rafter,
an occasional bounce-jump thrown in
for good measure. I grab a broom, thwack
the ceiling numerous times. The ruckus continues.

The sounds are not quite distinguishable, but
I think no human would frolic like that.
What is left after I eliminate humans? Of course,
raccoons and squirrels. I haven't seen a raccoon
in ages. That leaves squirrels, and the yard
is thick with the audacious little bastards.

I lug the waste basket outside to empty, and that's when I see a squirrel leap from the roof onto the dogwood tree. It's the end of February, and I'm rain-soaked, cold, but need to investigate.

I drag a ladder from the garage, climb to the roof, find six torn and shredded shingles. I see no hole through the plywood. The varmint clawed its way toward the chimney's warmth.

Tomorrow I will replace shingles. Tonight, however, I'm consulting my Betty Crocker cookbook for the best recipe for baked squirrel.

MY CATHOLIC BOYHOOD

First day at camp Saint Joseph I pretend
to participate in Catholic rituals.
My dad, a non-practicing Catholic,
never taught me proper procedures. I
am nine years old, not sure which knee
goes down first to genuflect, so I watch
other boys from the corner of my eye.
It looks as if only one knee is involved.
Safe so far. Father Mason sounds as if
he's singing for his own pleasure, but I
listen, baffled by his language. I don't
catch on to the sign of the cross either.
I simply dance my hand over my chest
a few time, and I'm through. If the boys
slow it down some, I can imitate.
Communion is a cinch. I fall to both knees
and stick out my tongue. The priest places
a wafer in my mouth that dissolves
faster than a breath mint. After church
one of the boys tells me we have to do
it all again in the evening. Twice a day!
Where's the cavalry when I need them?
I don't know the difference between mass
and communion, between a sacrament
and a sacrifice. Before the second dose
of church, I do find a tree my size near
the baseball diamond that I hide behind
without feeling egregious guilt or abhorrent sin.

USES OF A HOMEMADE TELESCOPE

I think of it as a personal device
that lets me snoop on my neighbors. It could
be used as a baton to conduct Gustav Holst's
Planets or as a celestial cattle prod. It might

be employed as a way, finally, to shrink politics
in Washington by viewing D. C. from the
opposite end of the scope, or could solve an
argument by having your antagonist look
through one end while you look through the

other, allowing both of you to see eye to eye.
What about a drum major twirling it in the
4th of July parade or pressed into service as
a gigantic hair curler? It's too insubstantial

to utilize as a tomato stake, but you might
want to focus it on the critters that devastate
your garden. It is the magic wand to
the stars, that is, a tool for gathering
intelligence about Hollywood celebrities.

How about those nights when your skin
is itchy? It becomes the ultimate back
scratchier. Lastly, for your annual checkup,
it is extremely handy for a quick colonoscopy.

And you thought there was only one way
to use it to get closer to the moon. How
heavenly wrong you were.

CATATONIC

Condemning cats is more controversial
then sex. Cat owners think their pets are
ultra human in spite of keening meows.
Cats detest water or to be picked up
unless they come to you. They can slaughter
a piece of cloth in no time, favorite
sharpening posts: couches and curtains.
They're consummate shower-rod walkers.

Their poop and pee reeks and lasts forever.
They're two of the most hellacious odors
in existence next to an eviscerated
decomposing body. Cats are notorious
for taking a dump in flower beds and famous
for triggering hysteria when the owner's
hands dig into soil and come up smelling
like rotten eggs or vomit.

Dogs need licenses. Why not cats? And,
where is the cat counterpart to a dog catcher?
I like a cat that acts like a dog, that smiles
at you now and then and wags its tail.
Have you ever tried to turn a cat over
and rub its belly? You'll end up with an arm
full of Band-Aids.

The best thing about cats is their self-containment.
With adequate water and food, they can
be left alone for several days to destroy
whatever they get their claws into.

Cats suffer from pica, an eating disorder
that causes them to view toilet paper as a culinary
delicacy, a mouthwatering treat, and they use
leftovers to decorate the bathroom.

I know I've been tough on cats, so let me say
there's nothing more adorable than a kitten
unless it's a pair of gloves or slippers made
from their fur.

DOGMATIC

Dogs are neurotic and unpredictable.
They also fart in mixed company.
Have you ever seen a cat wear a dress?
I've seen dogs done up as drag queens, or
was it the drag queens that were dogs?

When I was a boy, I used to take dogs
off the street. I could have my pick of
whatever came down the avenue.
We were our own dog catchers back then.

A stray hung around grandma's cottage
at Buckeye Lake. She claimed it smiled.
I didn't believe it until I saw it pull back its lips
in a big toothy grin. Eventually,
the dog disappeared, smile and all.

And then there was Aunt Ada who swore
her dog said mama. You see, dogs make people
hallucinatory.

Whenever I walk by a certain farm off a gravel
road in the Hocking Hills, a hound dog tied
to a doghouse turns a series of somersaults
as if taught by a trainer. I think the dog is

spastic, trying to take advantage of limited space
by taking to the air. Or else it's seen too many
episodes of *The Flying Nun.*

Dogs make good pets if you're in your second
childhood and enjoy running around the backyard
with a rubber ball.

Dogs are famous for hanging their heads out
car windows. They could start a lake with the
amount of drool and saliva flying from their mouths

Let's face it, dogs are great pets for pooping and peeing
on other people's lawns. Moreover, I ask you
what animal can better entertain by dragging its butt
across the carpet as if it were a two-legged chariot?

No matter how much a dog laps an owner's face,
a dog lover is never daunted by dog breath.

You must think by now I hate dogs, but I don't.
They perform many hygienic services
such as disposing of cat crap and sniffing
each other's rear.

I really can't talk against all dogs. I own one
that barks constantly, and this is the quietest
he's ever been since his return from the taxidermist.

GUNS GALORE

People are impressed with my gun collection,
meaning they probably have one hidden
under their belts. A single shot rifle, a Walther
P99, German semi-automatic pistol, a Colt
Diamondback, and a Colt single action army
revolver comprise my armory and constitute
part of my inheritance. In truth,

I know nothing about any of them except their
names. They lie like beached metal fish
in a plastic bag in the closet. I don't know
how to load them. I'd blow off my leg if
I tried. I guess I'd rather club an intruder
then shoot him. My friends drip

with more jealousy than Hera. When I've seen
their keen eyes covet, I've wanted to quote the
sixth commandment. What is it about guns
that compels people to want them?
Does possessing a gun fatten the ego,
inflate self-worth, or simply make a man
out of anyone who touches a trigger?
Women beware!

I've seen chest hair grow even as a man
caressed the stock of a Remington. If
you think you must have a gun, grow a beard
and get a musket. Just don't set the drapes on fire.

SOMETHING TO DO WITH RACCOONS

I first became aware raccoons were attempting
to appropriate my house the night I spotted one hanging
in the dining room window like a brown Christmas wreath.
I knew immediately where I would screw a seasonal bulb
if I had one. I pounded on the window like a drunk
locked out of his house. The varmint scrambled upward
past the overhang to the roof. I couldn't laugh off
the incident because something had destroyed shingles
the week before Now that I knew the culprit, I didn't want
to cause the animal misery, but if I had caught it,
I would have ripped its skin off and attached its tail
to the antenna of my car.

Next day, I set a trap with an apple as bait.
Before the night was over, I caught my raccoon
and, during the following week, four more. My cousin
transported the cage to the creek and turned the critters loose.

I'm beginning to think there are so many raccoons,
I should install a conveyor belt that runs from a nearby
patch of woods into the cage. That way, there would be
predictable forewarning of their invasion. On rainy days,
I'm tempted to crawl into the cage myself to escape
the drip drip drip from the kitchen ceiling where shingles
were shredded.

Since raccoons can use all five fingers like a human,
I'm thinking of signing them up for piano lessons,
an act I can take on the road and from which I can generate
additional income. If a muskrat can sing about love,
certainly a raccoon can learn to play Rachmaninoff.

DEAR LOUISE

Thank you for submitting your poems
to *Arse-Kicking Review*. Unfortunately
they do do not meet our current needs.
We apologize for the three-year wait
and for the condition of the poems
we are returning.

My wife spilled wine on poem number one,
hung it over the fireplace to dry,
and, unfortunately, it burned around the edges.
The middle, however, is still intact.

Poem number two was mistaken
for a bill and mailed to the electric
company. They would like to publish it
in their monthly newsletter, but I told them
they had to obtain your permission.

The third poem interested us, but
according to our guidelines you must submit
duplicates in Swahili. You might want
to try us again on that one.

The dog ate poem four. We offer our regrets
that Coco, our Chihuahua, found the fruits
of your labor so appetizing. No pun intended.

We were waiting for your poem to reappear
from Coco's posterior so we could forward it
to you, but our little Coco was washed away
in a flash flood.

Our seven-year-old son made an origami
dinosaur with poem number five, and we
unfolded it and are currently pressing out
the creases in the family Bible.
Will mail back when ready.

Thank you again for your submission.
I have enclosed a copy of our magazine
as recompense. I hope you enjoy
your Arse-Kicking experience.
Sincerely, Harry Legg, Editor.

IN THE PARLOR

When I was nine, my divorced mom dated
a barfly from Shadesville, a burg with several houses,
a gas station, and a beer joint. Martin, friend
of the barfly, died suddenly one July night
in a head-on car crash. He was embalmed and
displayed in his parents' clapboard house in Shadesville.
Nine-year-old curiosity did not include looking
at dead bodies, but Mom dragged me along.

The casket was almost as long as the room was wide.
The space reminded me of the inside of a streetcar.
Martin's face was powdered and looked younger
than his eighteen years. The overly sweet scent of
flowers nauseated me, and I wanted to race outside
into fresh air. Instead, I stared at Martin because
I'd never seen a dead person in someone's house before.
I kept looking back and forth between the maroon
and floral carpet and the corpse. Martin was tall,
but I couldn't see his shoes because the lower part
of the casket was closed.

It's not my way to lie, but I wanted to leave
so bad I said I had to pee when I didn't. I knew
Mom wouldn't allow me to use someone else's toilet,
so that meant we would soon depart. Of course,
we headed to the bar, but at least I didn't think
there would be any dead people there.

Inside the bar, I sat at a table clothed in colored light from the jukebox, occasionally offering a prayer over and over again, contrite but still believing that my need to pee was simply an act of God.

AMOROUS ADVICE

My friend, Chuck, says I won't bump elbows
with the right person in a bar.   The best I can do
won't be of my caliber. I'm flattered by
his high estimation of me, but at this point
I would descend into hell for romance.
It's hard to make someone else understand
the devil's flames are inconsequential
compared to living in a house without intimacy
or where no one but me leaves fingerprints
on a polished table.

Try church, he suggests, but how do I sort
people in a church when most are wearing pretense,
pomp, or self-blinders dipped in holy water?

I might try the internet. He likes that idea.
With my luck, however, I might spend a week
texting with a street walker or a gorilla
without knowing it.

My best bet is to write love letters to myself.
Dear Nik, I wish you much love, and someday
we may even be married.

All kidding aside, I tell him. I'm not young anymore.
I have to take what I can get. *Bullshit
and bones*, he barks. *You're an educated, talented man,
and you do not have to take what you get.*
I hear him, but it's not registering
in my disbelieving brain.

It's finally time for the showdown.
I tell him I plan to put myself up for sale
in a thrift store. With a crooked smile he says,
*Just remember to wear a blue tag.
Blue tag items are half price on Tuesdays.*

WRONG TURN

I'm lost among cornfields. I took a wrong turn
downtown heading toward a friend's house.
It is the kind of day you don't make songs about,
gray as a dolphin, gloomy as Halloween night,
my concern: how to get away from rural Ohio
and back toward the city.

Surrounded by silence, the only sound emanates
from the car's engine. Since I don't read the paper,
I don't know if rain will eventually turn to snow.
I keep looking for road signs, and there are few.
I have fallen down Alice's rabbit hole and don't
know where I will land.

The best plan is to call my friend and tell her
I am lost and will be late. After her humorous
interlude, because I am lost so close to home,
she insists on staying on the phone and directing
me.

I look in the mirror. I don't look frightened,
but my stomach is doing tumultuous somersaults.
I really am lost and don't know which direction
to turn next. I feel as if I am driving in a world
of nothingness, but she reassures me if I
identify at least one road sign, she can coach me
toward her house.

I have been more than an hour without knowing where I am. I could have swum the English Channel in less time. She knows the area, and after I identify one sign, she, meticulous as a seamstress, and after forty-five more minutes, leads me to her driveway. When I turn in, I feel as successful as an astronaut who has just orbited the earth which, in my estimation, wouldn't have taken as long.

AUNT CANDY CAPTIVATES THE NURSING HOME

Do I look my age, Aunt Candy asks. *I can't tell.*
All of my mirrors are coated with baby powder.
Fingers taper up to folds beneath her chin,
over-rouged cheeks growing redder. I'm not
embarrassed to say I'd look better with a face-lift.
A hand on either cheekbone, she cranks her face up
so tight it looks like she's swallowed a tube of
Preparation H. Her red Clara Bow lips make a cherry
look pale. What am I supposed to say to an
eighty-five-year-old woman in black leotards
and a skirt the length of a napkin?

I try to be fashionable. I think it cheers people up.
Don't you? I don't want to interrupt to say what
I'm thinking, that other residents are probably laughing
like hyenas at her 80s vintage dinosaur sweatshirt
and T-Rex high heels, so I smother a smile and say
she couldn't look lovelier.

I've saved her hair until last. It's the first thing you see
like a fire engine coming right at you. Only this isn't red.
It's yellow as egg yolk. The crowning touch, pun
unintended, is the style. It looks as if a flying saucer
has landed on her head with a bun on top and a tail
attached, the look from another planet.

She wobbles to her feet to see me out. The cane she lifts from beside her chair has a knob on top as big as a tennis ball embedded with rhinestones.

At the door she gives me a big smile that only unnerves me for a second before I realize they really are her teeth and not the wind-up kind that chatter and do a country western dance.

HAIRCUT

When I was a senior in high school,
a first-time barber hacked my hair.
I picked at it for weeks, unable to retain
my style, thinking I could make it longer
by manipulation.

Weeks rivered by without much growth.
I pulled hair together over a natural, center part,
pinned it with one of Mom's bobby pins,
hoping when I removed the pin, the part would
be gone. No such luck. The length just wasn't there.

During this time of my butchered bouffant,
students were scheduling to have their
senior pictures taken at a professional studio.
Wearing a hat was a temptation, but I continued
to pull hair over the part and into places
where I needed it.

The day of my scheduled appointment arrived.
I don't know which concerned me the most,
the imperfect knot in my tie or my coiffure.
I faked big hair as best I could and entered
the studio. The photographer placed me
and arranged lighting. Snap. And snap again.
The damage was done for all eternity.

Weeks later, I received proofs, and the first thing
I noticed was the irregular shape of my head.
Hair extended on one side six inches
from my face. Okay, I exaggerate a little, but
the protrusion was obvious.

A few more weeks passed, and it was time to
pick up the actual photographs. Lo and behold,
as I approached the shop, a picture of myself
stared back at me from the showcase window.
The photographer had put my picture on display
either as an example of his work or as an example
of a boy's chopped, chewed, and lopsided hairstyle.

A MODESTY PROPOSAL

The world needs to pay attention to me.
I'm completely successful, beating my
chest like a literary Tarzan to prove it.
There would be an uprising if I quit
writing. My red wheelbarrow is full
of masterpieces. Face it, you were born
to hunger after my poems, prostrate
yourself at the feat of my onomatopoeia.
Admire my alliteration, allude, awaken,
be astonished by my assonance. The
brilliance of my blank verse and formal
verse bedazzles, beguiles. My books belong
on your shelf. Bestow the bulk of your time
reading my words. Awaken to the wonder
of true talent. I caress my confidence
conjuring images as if from Houdini"s
hat. Carpe Me-um, Seize my couplets.
Conspire with my consonance. Shall I
offer you a conceit and compare myself
and my work to a summer's day? I can't
hide my hyperbole under a thousand
drafts of narrative genius any longer.
The truth is out, and I'm about to shout
and tout, no doubt, my expert rhymes.
Let's form a couplet, you and I. Open
your eyes of your cliché before it's too
late or you won't see the forest for the
metonymy.

POEM KILLERS

Muscles in my jaws tighten as speakers
around the table take turns critiquing
my poem. I had hoped my poem would be
a butterfly, but it must be a fly because
they're pulling its wings off. What poem
can survive scrutiny predicated on analysis?
The answer will surface next month
when the group dissects Psalm 23. If
the poem were a flower, being here
would be the difference between being
in a botany lab and a botanical garden.
Poetry isn't dead, but over the years it's
been maimed, maltreated, and massacred
by teachers who mistook explication
for appreciation. For a pedagogue, pleasure
from a poem constitutes a criminal act.
Dissection is the exorcism for entertainment.
If doggerel and Hallmark can satisfy
the masses, why can't a bona fide poem
be accessible to the majority? Teachers
and scholars remove muscle from a poem,
extract vertebra, devein its flesh, leave
an empty carcass of verse for academic
vultures. I'd like to see the day when
a teenage delinquent vandalizes

a library and escapes with all the poetry
he can carry. In retrospect, most teachers
should be flooded by shame for picking
the petals from the flower of poetry,
for relegating poetry to academia,
and ultimately ask, Oh, what have I done?

WORDS BY WHICH WE ARE KNOWN

We all carry identification with our name
printed on it as proof of who we are.
Otherwise, it would be troublesome to
say, Hey, you, and have the whole place
turn around and in unison answer, *Who, me?*
Albeit, some names make the forehead ache
with embarrassment. Try Archibald Appleslap
who early on turned himself into the name
police and became Hugo Smith.

Ever wonder why we have nicknames?
They serve as an escape hatch from appalling
appellations that shake a listener's ears.
What happens, though, when nicknames
exceed boundaries of the most liberal
imagination? Take three of my dad's
brother's nicknames for example: Rope,
Coffee Pot, and Big Sam. As years passed,
the neighborhood took those name for granted.

Sometimes nicknames derive from a distinguishing
body part like a big skull or a large rear
which, in that case, could lead to someone
being tagged as a Butthead.. My dad's height
elicited the byname of Shorty.
My sobriquet is Bud as in rosebud,
 the famous last word in Citizen Kane.

If you're fiercely opposed to your name,
don't suffer. Pick a body part or something
that sounds preposterous and reinvent yourself.
The world awaits the nonsense of your new name.

A POET'S PREROGATIVE

My cousin asks why I don't write
sunnier poems. I say, You mean the kind
that makes a person want to go to Florida?
His face drops as if misunderstood.
Something that lifts me up, he says.
My sarcasm hesitates, *You mean like
elevator poems.* He smirks dismay,
but keeps his face free of expression.

*I'm a poet. I'm supposed to be morbid,
but you must admit I do it with flare.*
He holds his hands out as if surrendering.
*That's my point. What you write about
seems so real. I think you're a closet
mortician. You mean that what I undertake
evokes?* This time he squeezes his hands
into fists.

I hang my head a little, feigning defeat.
He seems satisfied that he has vanquished
me, but I counter with verbal delight.
Then fire me as your personal poet.
He inhales a deep breath, stiffens his fingers
as if ready to conquer with a choke hold.
Standing up, he throws back his shoulders
and roars, *I give up!* Unable to suppress
my propensity for a perverse response,
I start for the door, turn, and say,
Then I'll go home and write about it.

WAITING ROOM

In the doctor's waiting room, I avoid
boredom by walking to the aquarium.
Goldfish, like pieces of sun with tails,
flit and turn, flit and turn. They have
no sky reflection to swim through,
and the coral looks scratchy. One fish
hides in a tangle of seaweed in the corner.
I pop out my cell phone for a picture.
Other people watch me as if I'm an
eccentric with blueberry stains on my face.
The photo shows a fish with its mouth
nearly pressed against the glass. It's
a comical shot like the fish is posing
or ready to kiss its own reflection.
I sit down, and the fish follows my
movement. I wonder how they endure
their limited environment ? Do any
ever reach a fish's old age? They
fatten, swim, and watch us in our
limited space the way God watches
us in our own small lives. A nurse
opens a door and calls my name
I rise and follow her, the fish
and philosophy already forgotten.

MY LIFE AS A SONGBIRD

I cannot trill r's. They simply walk
down my tongue too slowly. They lay
in my mouth flat as roadkill. The word
burro is my nemesis. After numerous
failures to trill it, I resort to the synonym
jackass. I've tried dozens of tongue
configurations until my tongue flies
in and out quick as an iguana's, but
that only stacks up r's until I've used
hundreds of tongue miles to no avail.
My tongue has become a frequent flier
without a destination. I've made a seesaw
of my tongue, practicing up and down
movement. It doesn't help. I've put
my tongue just below the roof of my mouth,
tensed my tongue, and blown air through my mouth
as the Duolingo manual instructed. The result
is a desktop full of spittle that dampens
enthusiasm. I've never been one to eject
saliva in mixed company. Is there
such a thing as a lip license? Maybe
that's what I need. As Tweety Bird would say,
It would be a real trill to trill. Right now,
as the canary flies, I'm a long way off.

DEMOLITION DERBY

At the Fairfield County Fair sunset pours
its rosy cellophane over the racetrack.
People are two and three deep at the fence,
before a packed grandstand.

A '64 Chrysler Imperial,
Crown Victoria, and Chevy Impala roar
onto the track like steel beasts. The youngest
driver,16 years old, tears his Imperial
as if he invented speed. All three monsters
rumble menacing threats A hint of moon
brightens the occasional backfire. Cars
pound each other, slam toward victory,
each on its verge of being bulldozed,
destroyed. Front wheel drive transforms
the Impala into a massive battering ram
that flattens the front of the Victoria.

I watch a sport that validates destruction,
anger, and pay back, that lets drivers
even the score. The full moon monopolizes
the sky, its light white as the red cross
vehicle visible on the sidelines. I don't stay,
but assume the 6.8 liter V8 Chrysler
freight-trained its way to the finish. I feign
interest to watch reactions to annihilation,
a rumbling excuse to redirect rancor.
Leaving, the moon is in overdrive.

SUBSTITUTE MAILMAN

Blue shorts accentuated the substitute
mailman's bowed legs as if he'd been
riding a horse for days across lawn
after lawn. Bouncing along with his
mailbag on his shoulder, he was
oblivious of a breeze catching letters
and sailing them under the neighbor's
ornamental shrubs.

Abe Johnson's income tax return flopped
under Janet Shirmir's wintergreen boxwood.
Jim Langley's overdue electric bill got
tangled in Virginia Vaserlee's arborvitae.
Guy Garrison's copy of Playgirl plunged
into Minnie Marlowe's maiden grass.

The exchange began. The whole neighborhood
undertook to deliver the appropriate mail to
the right person. People congregated on the
street. It was Beggar's night without bags
but with misplaced envelopes. People became
acquainted with one another. Friendships
bloomed. Romance blossomed.

Jameson Hughs received three different boxes, each addressed to a different person other than himself. He decided to forgo Christmas shopping and simply wrap these boxes instead of returning them to their rightful owners. It never did surface to whom he gave a bustier, an assortment of ladies' underwear, and six size D brassieres.

For over three weeks the substitute mailman lost, misplaced, and miss-delivered mail. Just as the scavenger hunt began to be accepted as daily entertainment, a new mailman appeared. He never miss-delivered one thing.

The neighborhood settled into regular routines again, but it's rumored that the substitute mailman bought a small farm in Southern Ohio and is now spreading manure instead of mail.

A MURDEROUS POET

One morning I awaken a murderous
poet who wants to kill the abstract words
of other poets. When asked to read
someone's work that lies like a verbal
shipwreck at the bottom of intellect
and imagination, I want to make no
apology for twisting the page
into nonexistence, crushing it down
to the size of a bubble gum wrapper.
I hate it more than doggerel when
a poem is not accessible, reachable,
attainable, approachable. I don't
mind working a little to understand,
but I don't want my guts kicked out
by the challenge of hieroglyphics
when I'm simply trying to read
and enjoy. I should shut up such biased
beliefs, but I won't. I will go on
explaining why the majority
of the American population hate
poetry. Poetry needs clarity,
words that meanings shine through,
clear as a Windexed window. Is there any
room in the genre for the obscure, arcane,
and esoteric, or a line such as the long

illiterate squirrel slowly curses herself
for laying down her gown on the gambling
table. Excuse me while I go to work
to interpret, polish, and send this to
a textbook publisher.

SPARE PART

I wheeled my Hyundai Genesis into
the parking lot of the hair salon and
pulled up to the curb. Before I could shut
off the engine or put the car into park,
my foot slipped, hit the accelerator,
and I flew into the handicapped
parking sign, smashing it flatter than
a table top. I sat stunned. Attracted
by the crash, people in the salon rushed
to the window to look at my mishap.
Embarrassed, I wanted to disappear.

I got out to asses the damage. A third
of the front end of my car lay on the
ground. How could I possibly be
nonchalant in disposing of it. I
casually lifted up the piece, almost
as big as a small Volkswagen, popped
the trunk, dropped the part into the
opening, and slammed the lid. I felt as
if I had just disposed of a murder victim.
The hole in the front end was so big
 I could see the entire wheel assembly,
and I wondered if I had a new way to
access the oil stick.

Because I didn't want to drive around
in what looked like a frame, the next
day, my brother taped the damaged
section back into place with silver
duct tape. The result looked as if my
car had racing stripes.

On the road I worried that a significant
bump might start parts flying. I
considered myself lucky that I didn't
have to tape a flashlight onto the hood
to replace a headlight.

As I roll down the street,
I'm everyone's joke. In the meantime
it's not I but my poor car that deserves
the handicapped space.

VOCAL MUSIC CLASS

Miss Bibler, my seventh grade music teacher,
thought I was singing, but I only moved my
mouth. I couldn't carry a tune. I refused
to embarrass myself by sounding off-key.
The only time I chimed in, pun intended,
was when we sang "Old McDonald's Farm."
I could quack quack here, quack quack there
with confidence. At Christmas time, during
"Up On the Housetop," I roared out *ho ho ho*.
Often I raised my music book just above my
mouth so she couldn't tell I wasn't singing.

Miss Bibler used a pitch pipe to get us started.
She blew into it as if she were summoning
the troops. I never understood how a pitch
pipe could help me sing, but the gadget
fascinated me, and I wondered if I listened
to it long enough, could I learn to sing?

Truth is, I really enjoyed music class,
particularly when she played recordings.
The first time I ever heard "Dance Macabre,"
she told us the story of goblins and ghosts
dancing until the fatal light of dawn.

Being unable to sing, I gave up the whole business and started to whistle. I whistled everything from the top ten hits to show tunes and movie soundtracks. My most ambitious undertaking was Rachmaninoff's second piano concerto in C minor, Opus 18 which, without any promise of Carnegie Hall, I'm still working on today.

MEDIA MESS

I no longer watch television or
subscribe to the newspaper. Lies and
slanted information have become the
norm. The hyped-up headline captures
imagination, dazzles curiosity, but when
the story is finally presented, its content
contains little more than repetition of the
headline.

News anchor repartee accounts for
at least a third of the broadcast. Tongues
spew out the same stories every night
with different names, dates, and places.

How can a whole hour's worth of content
have no substance? Should I care that
Kim Kardashian was attacked by bees?

The meteorologist, a harlequin who
dances from map to map, speaks
vernacular only another meteorologist
can understand. Mostly, I want
to know if it's going to rain. It's a
yes or no question. I sit through
another fifteen minutes of beating

around the bush, and then I hear
nimbostratus clouds will precipitate
indefinitely followed by more
precipitation from cumulonimbus, maybe.

Following the meteorological diatribe,
I employ a more reliable method of
determining the weather. I open the door
and look outside.

I'm even giving up the weather report. How
insulting to be told that wind blows and
rain is wet.

ASBESTOS

Mom, Aunt Liz, and I reach the end
of the dirt road leading from a relative's
cabin to the highway where our car is
parked. They refuse to get in immediately
because the car has trapped July heat.
We fling car doors open and remain
outside. They are absorbed in conversation.
I sight something on the gravel berm
that looks dead. At least it's not pulsating.
It's the color and shape of a gray mouse.
Moving closer, it becomes asbestos.
I can already see them shudder as I
burn with perversity. Carefully I
pick it up with two fingers the way I
would a real mouse. I turn and walk
in their direction. When they see what
I carry, they scream, and their faces go
white. Backing away, they plead for me
to stop. When they step back, I step forward.
It's a menacing dance, and I'm the threatening
leader, mocking their fear with *You guys
are afraid of a piece of asbestos!*
At first they're not convinced, voices
bordering on out and out screams. Soon,
they become angry and insist that I drop it,
which I do, but not without kicking it

toward them. They jump back, look at it,
hesitant to acknowledge their overreaction,
but relieved. The teasing child in me
gets in, closes the car door and waits
to receive his finger-wagging reprimand.

THE VALUE IN WAITING TO DIE

It is Saturday, and the whole country watches
football, the greatest molestation sport ever,
the pigskin excuse for ass grabbing. I am
desperate because the Buckeyes are losing,
so I decide to call the suicide prevention line.
The busy signal suggests another fan is watching
the Buckeyes. I wait ten minutes, consider
my options. Rope, knife, gun, gas, carbon
monoxide, and staring at row after row of zeros
in my checkbook are possibilities, but so many
choices make it as hard as picking out toilet paper.
Do I want thick, thin, plain, quilted, colored,
and if colored, what color? Store brand,
name brand? With or without images? Signed
or unsigned by the artist? By the time I complete
the mental catalog, it's time to redial, which I do,
only to receive a message that the number is
no longer in service and has been changed.

I dial the different number. I'm told
there will be a fifty-five minute wait and
asked if I want to be called when my turn in line
comes up? I choose to wait and listen to
messages of apology, words that tell me how
important I am, and reassurance that someone

who saves lives of football fans will soon be
on the line. All of this while Richard Strauss's
"Death and Transfiguration" plays in the
background. Suddenly, I see a snowbird land
on the windowsill, and I want to live. At this point,
a man answers and asks what he can do for me.
I hang up and think about how waiting has
kept me alive. So, until I'm in a sunnier mood,
and to guarantee myself an indefinite wait, I
Google the number for the Social Security office.

TALKING TO GOD

I'm awakened on the way up to heaven
by God's voice. How are you, she asks,
and I answer, I'm just stopping by.
That's what you think, she says. I got big plans
for you. How big? I ask. As big as the sky,
she tells me. Well, I'm not planning to stick
around for all that. In fact, it's so high up here
I think I'm going to have a nose bleed.
Oh, no. We can't have anything red up here.
That belongs down below. Stick a piece of cloud
in each nostril, she advises, and you'll be fine.
I don't mean to be belligerent, but I think
I'll be on my way. Hasta luego. Do you speak
Spanish, God inquires. Actually, I'm Italian.
I just happen to know a couple Spanish phrases.
Do you speak Italian? God wants to know.
No, but I was asked to join the mafia
when I was a freshman in college. Do you
have any mafia members up here? They've
all gone to hell, God says with a satisfied smile.
Why don't you settle in and make yourself
more comfortable. One of my angels has a robe
that will just fit you. I don't think so, I say.
Hard to get something around my pot belly.
Plus, I have my own sleepwear at home. This
is your new home, God informs me. You've

got to be kidding. Where's all the furniture?
Where's my writing desk? We do everything
on clouds up here, she answers. Am I dead?
I finally ask. Yes, she says. Otherwise we
wouldn't be having this chat. My eyes roll
in my head, and I start looking around frantically.
What is it you're searching for? God wants to know.
I'm hunting for a fire escape, I confess. That,
my dear man, is also down below.

OCTOGENARIAN ONE-STEP

Fifteen band members tune up and prepare
to revive Swing. The first set starts with
"Boogie Woogie Bugle Boy." Shoulder bare,
in three-inch heels, a shriveled woman struts
onto the dance floor. A man trails behind
her. Fossilized, the couple begin the East
Coast Swing. Five other couples coax their bodies
to the floor, motor control and coordination
cautious. The men wear pot bellies and pants
up to their armpits. They bend the women,
frail as spider webs, backwards, never to return.
A wheezing ambiance abounds. Song ended,
they all drop into chairs. "Sing, Sing, Sing" brings
the same bunch to the floor. They flaunt flashy
moves learned sixty years earlier, forfeit
finesse for balance, turning old age into
Collegiate Shag and Lindy Hop. Harnessing
limited energy, they hitch themselves
to high-stepping rhythms. By the end
of the dance, reddened faces resemble
football players coming off the field.
With damp foreheads, they claim disintegrating
partners and await the next dance.

FIRST FLIGHT

The night I boarded the plane for Europe,
I had three drinks and a tranquilizer.
I was full of things to say, but thought better
of opening my slurred mouth. The friend
I traveled with had no fear of falling,
but I did. Being claustrophobic,
I insisted on sitting near the window,
so I could see all the space I needed.

My friend seated herself beside me,
understanding that I wanted distraction,
and began jabbering about collecting
miniature trains. I could give a hoot
about trains, but the chatter kept my
mind off 35,000 feet in the air..

Friends had suggested ways to handle
fear of flying. I found the solution
when the hostess trooped down the aisle
with Bombay Sapphire Gin.

I asked questions I didn't need answers to
just to keep my mind occupied. I assumed
thinking about death was a natural part of flying,
and I became quickly adept at picturing various

descents. Of course, there was always the water
and sharks scenario. I thought of the old cliche
I was born to die, and that only made me love life
a little more.

I was doing okay until the plane started to rip
through turbulence. I felt as if I were surfing on
a tumultuous sea. My stomach rippled out the
first words of my epitaph when the plane leveled
off again, and we sped along smooth as a
sleight-of-hand trick.

After that scare and before we landed in Amsterdam,
I stopped the hostess for another Bombay Sapphire Gin,
the blissful ride that would have gotten me there
even without a plane.

TIME OUT

Early in my career I took time away
from teaching, worked as a technical writer
at North Electric, a Swedish company
in Galion Ohio. I drove a gas-guzzling
Oldsmobile Cutlass 442 that loved gas stations.
Because I commuted sixty miles each day,
the Cutlass roared into Marathon each evening
when I re-entered Columbus.

I hated to write narratives explaining how
to operate industrial-size telephone equipment.
Given a blueprint and time allotment, I was free
to organize my time anyway I wanted.
I didn't know how to read blueprints and
didn't want to learn. I faked reading them,
finished with days' worth of time to kill. I wrote
poetry undercover, kept my legal pad hidden
from my office mate whose Pinocchio nose finally
discovered my jottings. When the boss ambled by
and bent over my desk, I quickly flipped the pages.
In addition to poetry, I actually sharpened pencils
to pass time, took a book from the company library
on how to speak Swedish.

The next time the boss entered our outhouse-size
cubicle, I addressed him as Herr Sterrett. He answered,
Din shotty och felaktiga arbeten saknar market.
(Your shoddy and inaccurate work misses the mark.)
Was he telling me I wasn't right for the job?

He never did fire me, but one day right
after I handed in some of my work, I heard
him at the end of the building let out an
ear-splitting scream.

On Christmas Eve when we had to stay
until 5:30, I offered my resignation
wrapped in colorful paper with a bow,
thanked him for his efforts to tame me,
and beelined back to Columbus ready to kiss
the floor of my next teaching job
even if I got a lip full of splinters.

A LITTLE WALK NEVER HURT ANYONE

When I was little and wore a harness
to keep me located, Mom used to walk
beside me and admonish not to step on
sidewalk cracks for fear it would break
her back. That, of course, is an old
superstition with no validity.

On the other hand those same cracks
were my nemesis. Why couldn't I walk
without stumbling? It seemed as if every
crack in the sidewalk challenged my
equilibrium.

At four years old, I frequently folded
and skinned my ginglymus, which is a
fancy word for knee and adds a bit
of dignity to my story about
clumsiness. Maybe I walked too stiff
legged, or maybe I had already developed
a poet's mind whereby I became preoccupied
with details around me, oblivious of balance.

Mom gave me a slight tug and pulled me
along like a docile puppy to my next point
of upset. I prided myself if I could reach
a destination without flattening out on

concrete. Fissures, crevices, breaks may as well have been cliff edges. Maybe my body parts didn't fit together right. I felt as vulnerable as a marionette without strings.

I can say that nothing ever happened to Mom's spinal column as a result of my stepping on a fault, but I firmly believe the superstition should be revised to include scraped knees as well as bruised self-esteem.

Years passed, and I still step around cracks on a sidewalk, grateful to be upright and shrugging at my gullibility.

DOG IN THE RAIN

The neighbor is walking his mouse-size dog.
I can't identify the breed. It doesn't look
like a Chihuahua from the outside, and I
assume all dog parts are the same inside.
I want to stop the neighbor and ask him if
he was drinking when he picked out the dog,
or was he trying to pull a joke on his wife
who expected him to bring home a mastiff
the size of their backyard shed?

It starts to drizzle, and he picks up the dog,
puts it into his pocket. Just kidding.
Actually, that's what I expected him to do,
but instead, he pulls out a yellow slicker
and fits it over the unnameable dog. I
want to laugh, but I know he's proud of
his pup.

The dog, we'll call it Marsha and assume
it's female, although I don't know
if it is female or male since the bits and
pieces of it are too small to tell. Even so,
a gurgle of a laugh if insinuating itself up
my throat because the dog is frozen rigid
in its new attire. Marsha refuses to move,

stiff as the proverbial board. At that moment
it would pass as a bird dog pointing rigidly
west. If Marsha had come equipped with
wheels, he could tow her home like a Fisher
Price pull toy.

He has two options. He can pick her up,
carry her home, and place her on his car
as a hood ornament or remove the raincoat,
risk that rain will further reduce her size,
and mail her back in an envelope
to the pet shop, claiming that the dog he
bought came with a shrink-proof guarantee.

OPEN MIC

Welcome to the open mic portion
of our program. Since rules are well known,
I won't repeat them, but I will remind you
of the two-minute time allotment. Before
we begin, I want to present brief notes
about tonight's six readers.

Beatrice Bumfelt, an expert in speed reading,
brought a twenty-four page narrative
which she will attempt to read in two minutes.

You may remember Shorty Wire's mishap
from last week when he took open mic
literally, brought a screwdriver, unsealed
the cover, had screws loose by the end
of the reading, and received finger burns.
He's back this week with a different conflagration.

Xavier Kennelworth assumed doggerel meant
poetry about dogs. The Kennel Club has accepted
his poem for Puppy Poetry Paper, a weekly publication.

Our fourth reader, Sara Sweetheart, continues
her affiliation with Hallmark and brings us a piece
from her new chapbook, "I Love You, Truly."

Travis Airsick, world traveler, will read
the miraculous condensation of the social,
political, and religious practices of seven
continents in one haiku.

Lastly, W.D. McGriffith will depict the history
of his family from births to deaths in a series
of Petrarchan sonnets.

Oh, one final note: Lucy Layaside has lost
her found poem and will not be reading tonight.

Good luck to all the readers. To the audience,
may your patience bear the brunt.

LOGISTICS OF BUYING A NEW CAR

I'm unbuttoning my shirt, literally taking it
off my back as I walk into the car dealership.
A young salesman approaches me, trim and
suave, enough product in his hair to cut my
hand or survive a hurricane. I give him my
shirt and tell him I'm interested in buying
a new car. He tells me I have to give up
my belt and shoes too, since there's been
a recent increase in prices.

I really do need a car, so in stocking feet
I approach a vehicle that interests me, ask
how much the frame is? He says that they
start at twenty thousand. I ask him about
the cost of the body, and he says that would
be another twenty. At that price I inquire
whether he would throw in a steering wheel
and seats, but he is adamant that they are
extras and have to be negotiated. It seems
like a reasonable deal, so I tell him I'll
take it for a test drive once it's put together.

We gravitate toward his desk, and I begin
to sign more papers then I did when I bought
my house. After the twenty-fifth signature,

the pen runs out of ink, and he produces a rubber stamp with only a giant X on it. Before I get up, he says if I desire headlights and a heater, we can discuss that at some future time. He seems thrilled with his sale, and from beneath his desk he produces a suitcase in which I can carry my monumental stack of papers. He wishes me well, and I walk into the brightness of the day a happy man to have retained my skivvies.

PRIDE AND PERSPIRATION

I want to sweat like other boys
riding the bus to Camp Saint Joseph.
It is hot as the Serengeti plain,
and these boys have dots of water beneath
their nose. Under my twelve-year-old nose,
dry as a coconut shell, a few zits
redden my skin, but no sweat.

How can I become a man if I don't sweat?
Even my armpits are dry as a newly diapered baby.
I am losing confidence. I need to sweat.
If I had access to water, I would douse myself
and fake it. Who ever heard of a man who didn't
sweat?

Maybe something is wrong with my glands.
I'll have to read up on it in Mom's doctor book
when I get home.

In the meantime, there is always church.
I could pray for sweat or ask father Johnson
how he got his.

Some boys sweat in the back of their pants.
Unbelievable! A couple of them have a mustache
and sweat!

It just doesn't seem fair to grow up without sweat.
I've even seen nuns sweat between Hail Marys.
Why doesn't anyone ever talk about sweat?
People just seem to take it for granted.

My dad is a master sweater: face, chest,
even his wrists participate.

There is hope that when I die and I'm lying
in my coffin, the priest will make a man of me
by sprinkling holy water in all the right places.

BARGAIN RATE

I'm sitting at the bar. The only other person is
the bartender when she comes through the door
with a greeting as if she knows me. I never saw
this stout, middle-age woman in my life.
She grasps me in a hug and asks why I haven't called,
starts prattling about a cycle outside that she's trying
to get ten for. I'm picturing a Harley-Davidson CVO
Limited or something with handlebars in the air,
me holding them as if airing my armpits.
She keeps repeating ten, and I keep thinking ten
isn't a bad price for CVO Limited. She entices
the bartender to go outside and take a look.

When he returns, I can't tell anything from his
nonchalance and taciturn attitude, but he shakes
his head yes. She insists that I, too, come take a look.
In any case ten grand is a lot to pull out of a pocket,
but I follow her, suspicious about being alone
with a person who claims to be sleeping in her car
and to be an old friend of mine.

The whole scene is bizarre, but to keep things
moving, I follow her. Lo and behold, there
before my eyes is the much-lauded sale item,
a worn out Roadmaster Bicycle she is

asking ten dollars for. I fish in my pocket for
loose bills, give them to her. I'm now
the owner of a bicycle that I don't know what
to do with. I can't transport it in my sports car,
nor do I want it.

I walk back into the bar, announce to the bartender
he is now the proud owner of a bicycle. He accepts
the gift and wheels it indoors.

Now that negotiations are finished, I attempt to escape.
She follows me outside, and as I step toward my car,
bellows after me, *Don't forget, I'm bisexual.*

CLEAN

I own the cleanest credit cards in town,
and keys and coins and dollars, having spun
them through the washer by mistake.
Some anal fanatics would applaud my
cleanliness, but trust, sanitation was purely
an accident.

Recognition occurred the afternoon I reached
into my pocket to pay the snow-removal man.
Pockets empty, I remembered a pair of Levi's
still in the washer. Sure enough, they had gone
the cycle, rinsed, and wrapped around the agitator
tight as a rock climber's hand on the next rock.

Embarrassed, I excused myself, slipped into the
bedroom, spread the contents onto the bed, and
assessed the damage. Coins shone brighter,
Andrew Jackson's face scrubbed clean as a new bill.
I still had the magnetic strip on the cards to worry
about. Would any machine read them now that they
had been through a tsunami?

I strolled through the house to the snow-removal man
who waited, patient as a trained dog, at the back door.
With a diffident look, I handed him two damp twenties
and, hoping he wasn't an undercover cop,
asked if he accepted laundered money.

AT WAR WITH WHITE CASTLE

I shock the chef by requesting four
cheeseburgers without meat. His face
slackens in surprise, surrenders to
accommodation, claims he can do that.
I ask for extra pickles and onions, and
he casts me a look that says he thinks
I'm a visitor from the moon, becomes
fully flummoxed when I threw in a
last-minute request for a large order
of onion chips to put on my sandwiches.
His blank expression tells me I've
clouded comprehension. Popeye biceps
bulge with tattoos, broadcast potential
belligerency, so I put aside a request for
a Singapore Sling and settle for water.

I sit on a plastic chair and wait for my order,
study an enlarged photograph on the wall
of three young flappers from the 1930s
frocked in fur-collared coats and fedora,
bowler hats. Each lady holds a White Castle
sandwich. I don't know why the photo
fascinates me, except the girls seem
extremely satisfied to be eating only
U.S. government inspected meat.

The server announces my order.
His expression tells me I owe him big time.
I watch him watch me pick up the tray,
his smirk barely hidden. Over my shoulder
I say, *You're safe. On the moon we don't eat
beef or well-developed brawn.*

LESSONS IN SATISFACTION

*How to have dinner across the table
from a former lover behaving like a jerk.*
After you first arrive and sit down, say
something disparaging about their clothes.
Next, accidentally with all intent, kick the hell
out of their shins with heels they would swear
are stilettos. When the waiter arrives,
speak only French but order Italian.
During the meal, develop numerous ticks.
A twitching face or a clumsy hand are
excellent choices. Allow your trembling
paw to drop a spoon into the minestrone
then summon the waiter to fish it out.
Burp and develop hiccups. Tell them
the only way, according to your late
grandmother, to get them to subside is to
recite the Gettysburg Address. Begin
reciting between hics and cups until
a bout of choking sets in. Retrieve your
napkin, and red-faced, drop the cloth into
what's left of the minestrone. As you see
the waiter approach with the bill, throw your
arms into the air with helpless defeat,
claiming that you left your wallet at home.

Can you borrow enough to pay your part,
or is this lunch a surprise gift from the
cringing person shrunken into near
non-existence sitting across from you?
Finally, as you rise to leave with a final belch,
inquire whether the other party
would like an autograph.

MOBY'S

My bad seed sprouts at six-years-old.
Aunt Mary, Mom, and I are in Moby's
department store downtown. Mom's bogged down
with armsful of sale dresses, her back to Aunt Mary
and me. The place is crowded, people climbing walls
to get to sale items. Aunt Mary is facing four drawers
of ribbons. She's bending over the lowest drawer,
handsful of ribbons. Suddenly her dress flies
over her head. With her hands loaded, she can't
pull it down. Mom turns around, sees what's
happened, takes me by the arm, and starts fanning
my butt. Another customer sees Mom and says,
Just look how she's treating her child! Mom says,
*Lady, mind your own business. You didn't see
what he did!* And continues swinging. It's
difficult for her to hit the target, since I'm
wearing a harness with a lead on it that's now
dragging the floor. Aunt Mary pulls her dress
down, face red as a signal at a railroad crossing.
I'm crying, but I'm not abashed, and this,
of course, before the time when the prevalence
of pants became my saboteur.

NECKS

Aunt Betty says you can tell a person
has aged by the look of the neck.
My nineteen-year-old hand goes to mine
as if to cover the truth. We're parked,
about to go into the theater and see
Never on Sunday.

After the movie, back in the Impala,
she says it was about fast-walking
whores and good music. My hand
wants to check my neck.
We sit for awhile with the windows down.
Night is balmy and beset by bugs!
How do you know about necks? I ask.
Well, just look around, she answers.
Some old people's necks look like accordions.
I think of the movie, Jules Dassin,
and the squeezebox. Is she telling me
that someday my neck will look
like a concertina? Staring at her neck,
I don't see an accordion or even a fold.

We start home, theme from the movie
humming in my head. From the corner
of my eye, I'm watching her throat, its
slow movement when she talks, wondering
if the vocal cords are where it all starts.

HOW TO SURVIVE IN THE HOSPITAL

Refrain from pressing the red call button.
Nurses hate gossip sessions interrupted
by patients. Compliment doctors on bow ties and
snazzy dress. Try not to look dumb when they lapse
into medical terminology or golf jargon. Don't ask
about a release date, Only the custodian knows that.
Keep the barf bag well concealed, so none of the
kitchen staff sees it. In desperation, refrain
from teeth marks in the menu, although it's a
suitable substitute for food you've already hidden
under the bed. When the overweight respiratory
therapist walks through the door, try not to gawk
and gasp. You can tell from his heavy breathing
he's having a hard day too. Don't punch a hole
in the wall of the room next door to grab the neck
of the loquacious, obnoxious, audacious, loud-mouth,
know-it-all night owl who's kept you awake for the
last twelve hours. Your insurance won't cover idiocy.
Don't make balloons from rubber gloves and expect
a party. That's what's going on in the conference room.
Stay away from the main desk. It is the mother ship
manned by members who make a career of walking
in circles. Along with other souvenirs, pack
hospital washcloths and towels carefully in the bottom
of your duffel bag. Metal detectors do not detect clothe.
Finally, on the day of release when they say they have
sent for a wheelchair, point to a window
and tell them you know a faster way to escape.

DON'T TOUCH THE COWS

Cows should be in the pasture not on buns.
I believe nothing with a brain should be
eaten. That leaves some humans susceptible
to cannibalism. I am not a vegan.
I am a variable vegetarian. I can bear pig
on pizza because it's harder to sympathize
with swine, although a baby pig smells like
walnuts and is as cuddlesome and appealing
as a puppy. The *pig*-mentation of a porker's
iris does not, however, elicit sympathy.
Cow eyes, brown as a teddy bear's, engender
immediate empathy.

It's interesting that out of thousands
of burger ads the word cow is never mentioned.
It's always about beef. I believe the general
public has an unconscious guilt about eating
animals. That is why we never hear or read
about cow burgers. Anyone who disagrees
would be telling a whopper. Can you really
in good conscience picture a little dogie
as a double-decker or partake of a one-year-old
calf in Veal Parmesan? The meatball atop your
spaghetti might have once been someone's
pet. We wouldn't think of eating a dog

burger or a cat casserole, so why steer cattle
toward their fate at McDonald's? I don't want
to ear anything that has a heart, with the exception
of celery.

So, let's let the cattle alone.
Moreover, if you are at all existential,
you've already given the cows permission
to eat you too. If anyone is in disagreement,
now is the time to leave and take your beef
sandwich with you. Okay?

DESTINATION GOODWILL

Every couple of years at our house
Mom and her sisters conducted an
impromptu rummage sale with bags of
abandoned clothing and shoes earmarked for
Goodwill. Mom's house was the central location
where all the goods were brought before loading
them into one car. The hitch, however, was that
the stuff never made it to Goodwill.

It all began when they started to sift through
each other's belongings. What one person
was giving away, another person prized.
It didn't turn into a free-for-all, but one year,
for example, Mom ended up with two pairs
of Aunt Betty's shoes. Aunt Betty offered
Aunt Ada ten dollars for a fur stole. Aunt
Ada acquired a leather pocketbook from
Aunt Mary. Aunt Mary traded Aunt Liz
a winter coat for a pair of wool slacks.
Aunt Liz gave Aunt Laura four blouses.

They poked around in each other's sacks
for over an hour. The living room became
a dressing room. Aunt Mary had one leg
in her wool slacks at the same time Aunt

Laura buttoned up one of her new blouses. Mom was using her finger to squeeze a foot into Aunt Betty's shoe. Aunt Betty sat on the sofa with the fur stole draped around her shoulders as if Aunt Ada might renege on the deal. Even though it was June, Aunt Liz seemed comfortable in her winter coat.

At the end of the visit, all bags were filled with new acquisitions and, of course, nothing remained to donate to Goodwill. Anyone viewing the situation from the outside would have thought it was sale day at Macy's when anything you can get your hands on is yours. These ladies had turned shopping among themselves into a family art that only James Thurber could appreciate.

GOD LOVES GROUNDHOGS

They amble like brown, bloated, sweeper bags
across the backyard toward the shed, their fur
gleaming in sunlight. They've dug three holes
under the shed that lead to various tunnels.
At least once a day they come out to sun
themselves and flaunt their audacious egos.
I keep thinking I can get rid of them,
but nothing has worked. One radio announcer
suggested feeding them bubble gum.
They gobbled the gum and went on grazing.
The one I assume is the mother herds her young
to the adjacent churchyard each day to munch
wild grasses and dandelions. I've filled in
their holes, but they dig them right back out.
I would consider that laughable, except
they destroyed my last shed by eating up
through the floor.

As tempted as I have been, I do not reach
for a gun when I see them sunning themselves
atop the stone pile. After all, they are God's
creatures, but I wish he would take them back
to where he got them. The neighbor's cat prances
past the groundhog holes every night,
apparently not looking for a good fight.
On the other hand, the non-suicidal groundhogs,
ill-equipped to kill, stay in their hideouts.

Let's face it. I have a cage, and I'm catching them one by one, taking them to a distant creek, and turning them loose. Hopefully, I will be rid of he pests before their tunnels reach Fort Knox or before they ingest my entire shed.

Dr. R. Nikolas Macioci earned a PhD from The Ohio State University and taught English, Writers' Seminar (a course he created for select students), and Drama in Columbus City Schools. OCTELA, the Ohio Council of Teachers of English, awarded Nik Macioci best secondary English teacher in the state of Ohio.

He won First Place in the l987 National Writer's Union Poetry Competition judged by Denise Levertov, First Place in The Baudelaire Award Competition sponsored by The World Order of Narrative and Formalist Poets (1989). Second Place in Zone 3's first annual Rainmaker Awards, judged by Howard Nemerov (1989), and Second Place in the Writer's Digest annual competition, Judged by Diane Wakoski (1991).

Nik is the author of two chapbooks, *Cafes of Childhood*, and *Greatest Hits*, as well as five books: *Cafes of Childhood* (the original chapbook with additional poems), *Why Dance?*, *Necessary Windows*, *Mother Goosed* and *Occasional Heaven*. Forth-coming is *Rough*. His book, *Cafes of Childhood* was submitted for the Pulitzer Prize. Critics and judges called *Cafes of Childhood* a "beautifully harrowing account of child abuse, but not "sentimental" or self-pitying" an "amazing book," and "a single unified whole." In addition, Nik's work has been published in more than two hundred magazines here and abroad. Most recently, Macioci has published in *The Society of Classical Poets journal*, *Concho River Review*, *The Comstock Review*, *Blue Unicorn*, and *Chiron Review*. He is a member of Bistro poets critique group.

www.ingramcontent.com/pod-product-compliance
Lightning Source LLC
Chambersburg PA
CBHW030344100526
44592CB00010B/813